D0534678

'Tis what I feel, but can't define,
'tis what I know, but can't express.

—O. HENRY *(1862-1910)*
American writer

 Printed in the United States of America. Canadian representatives: General Publishing Co., Ltd., 30 Lesmill Road, Don Mills, Ontario M3B 2T6. International representatives: Worldwide Media Services, Inc., 115 East Twenty-third Street, New York, New York 10010. ISBN 0-89471-512-7 (paper). Cover illustration by Toby Schmidt. Interior illustrations by Marie Garafano. This book may be ordered by mail from the publisher. Please add $2.50 for postage and handling. *But try your bookstore first!* Running Press Book Publishers, 125 South Twenty-second Street, Philadelphia, Pennsylvania 19103.

LOVE

There is only one kind of love, but there are a thousand different versions.

—*FRANÇOIS DE LA ROCHEFOUCAULD (1613-1680)*
French moralist

I do love I know not what;
Sometimes this, and sometimes that

—*ROBERT HERRICK (1591-1674)*
English poet

In love, everything is true, everything is false; it is the one subject on which one cannot express an absurdity.

—*NICHOLAS CHAMFORT (1741-1794)*
French writer

Love is the only game that is not called on account of darkness.

—*THOMAS CARLYLE (1795-1881)*
Scottish writer

Sometimes it's a form of love just to talk to somebody that you have nothing in common with and still be fascinated by their presence.

—*DAVID BYRNE, b. 1952*
American entertainer

Among those whom I like or admire, I can find no common denominator, but among those whom I love, I can: all of them make me laugh.

—*W.H. AUDEN (1907-1973)*
American poet

But to see her was to love her,
Love but her, and love her for ever.

—*ROBERT BURNS (1759-1796)*
Scottish poet

Many a man has fallen in love with a girl in a light so dim he would not have chosen a suit by it.

—*MAURICE CHEVALIER (1888-1972)*
French entertainer

To live is like love, all reason is against it, and all healthy instinct for it.

—*SAMUEL BUTLER (1835-1902)*
English writer

I loved not yet, yet I loved to love . . .
I sought what I might love, in love with loving.

—*SAINT AUGUSTINE (354-430)*
Early Christian Church father

. . . the courage to share your feelings is critical to sustaining a love relationship.

—*HAROLD H. BLOOMFIELD, b. 1944*
American psychiatrist & writer
ROBERT B. KORY, b. 1950
American lecturer

Grow old along with me!
The best is yet to be,
The last of life for which the first was made.

—*ROBERT BROWNING (1812-1889)*
English poet

In many ways doth the full heart reveal
The presence of the love it would conceal.

—*SAMUEL TAYLOR COLERIDGE* (1772-1834)
English writer

. . . what I do
And what I dream include thee, as the wine
Must taste of its own grapes.

—*ELIZABETH BARRETT BROWNING (1806-1861)*
English poet

In love the paradox occurs that two beings become one and yet remain two.

—*ERICH FROMM (1900–1980)*
American psychoanalyst

In any relationship in which two people become one, the end result is two half people.

—*WAYNE DYER, b. 1940*
American writer

Love does not begin and end the way we seem to think it does. Love is a battle, love is a war; love is a growing up.

—*JAMES BALDWIN (1924–1987)*
American writer

The proof that experience teaches us nothing is that the end of one love does not prevent us from beginning another.

—*PAUL BOURGET (1852-1935)*
French writer

Love alone is capable of uniting living beings in such a way as to complete and fulfill them, for it alone takes them and joins them by what is deepest in themselves.

—*PIERRE TEILHARD DE CHARDIN (1881-1955)*
French paleontologist & philosopher

Where love is concerned, too much is not even enough!

—*PIERRE-AUGUSTIN CARON DE BEAUMARCHAIS (1732-1799)*
French playwright

The only true gift is a portion of yourself.

—*RALPH WALDO EMERSON (1803-1882)*
American writer

Can there be a love which does not make demands on its object?

—*CONFUCIUS (551-479 B.C.)*
Chinese philosopher

Love distills desire upon the eyes,
love brings bewitching grace into the heart . . .

—*EURIPIDES* (*c.* 484-406 B.C.)
Greek playwright

When love is good it can make you fly. Winning it is worth the risk. People fall in love and glow for weeks.

—*GEORGE DAVIS, b. 1939*
American writer & teacher

When I was very young I fell deeply in love . . . and really believed I would never feel that way again . . . then nine years later . . . I did, and much, much more strongly and deeply than before.

—*ISAK DINESEN (1885-1962)*
Danish writer

Oh love, as long as you can love.

—*FERDINAND FREILIGRATH (1810-1876)*
German poet

We find rest in those we love, and we provide a resting place in ourselves for those who love us.

—*SAINT BERNARD* OF *CLAIRVAUX (1090-1153)*
French ecclesiastic

Ideally, couples need three lives;
one for him, one for her, and one for them together.

—*JACQUELINE BISSET, b. 1946*
English actress

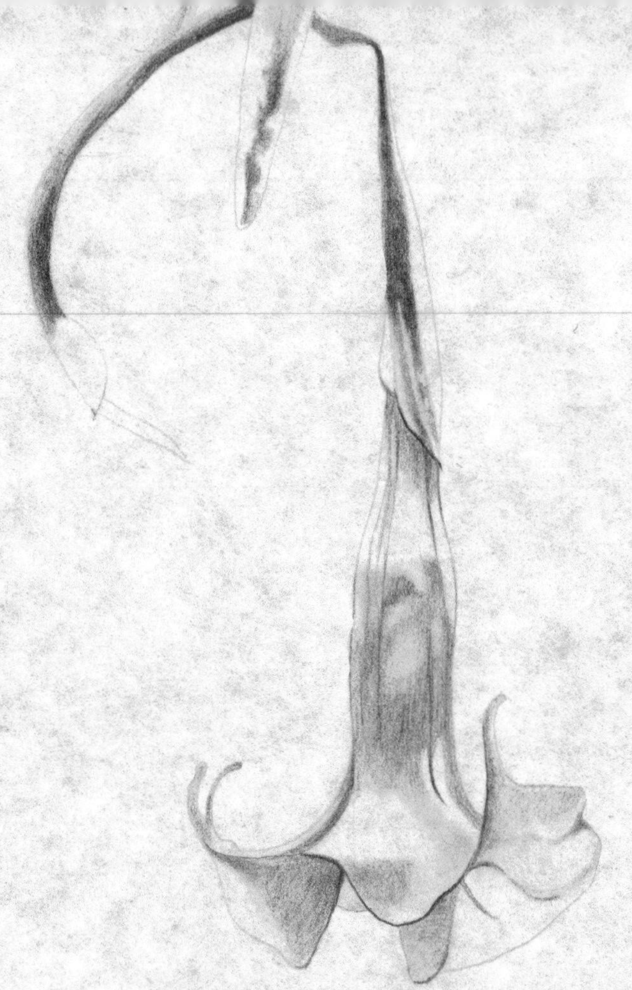

. . . if you love somebody,
tell them.

—*ROD McKUEN, b. 1933*
American poet

I like not only to be loved,
but to be told I am loved.

—*GEORGE ELIOT (1819-1880)*
English writer

We love the things we love for what they are.

—*ROBERT FROST (1874-1963)*
American poet

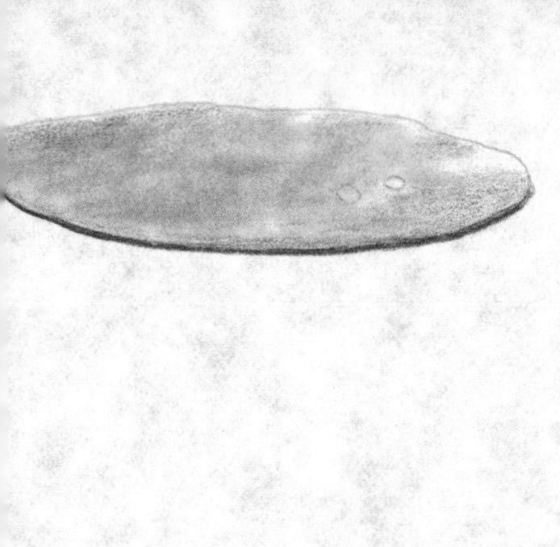

Immature love says: "I love you because I need you."
Mature love says: "I need you because I love you."

—*ERICH FROMM (1900–1980)*
American psychoanalyst

There is always something left to love. And if you ain't learned that, you ain't learned nothing.

—*LORRAINE HANSBERRY (1930-1965)*
American playwright

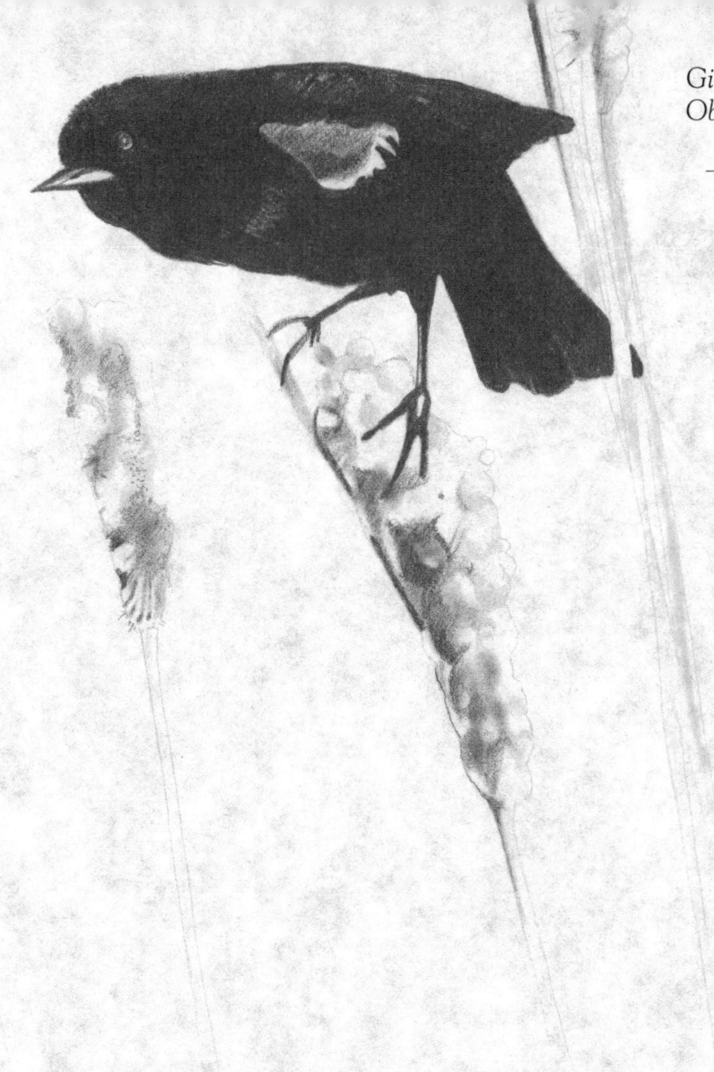

Give all to love;
Obey thy heart . . .

—*RALPH WALDO EMERSON (1803-1882)*
American writer

To love for the sake of being loved is human;
but to love for the sake of loving is angelic.

—*ALPHONSE DE LAMARTINE (1790-1869)*
French poet

To love is to place our happiness in the happiness of another.

—*G.W. LEIBNIZ (1646-1716)*
German philosopher & mathematician

Harmony is pure love, for love is complete agreement.

—*LOPE DE VEGA (1562-1635)*
Spanish writer

Love is . . . an endless mystery,
for it has nothing else to explain it.

—*RABINDRANATH TAGORE (1861-1941)*
Indian writer

Have all the keys removed from your typewriter except the ones needed to spell her name.

—ANONYMOUS

First romance, first love, is something so special to all of us, both emotionally and physically, that it touches our lives and enriches them forever.

—*ROSEMARY ROGERS, b. 1932*
American writer

Gratitude looks to the past and love to the present . . .

—C.S. *LEWIS (1898-1963)*
English writer

Love is supreme and unconditional; like is nice but limited.

—*DUKE ELLINGTON (1899-1974)*
American composer & bandleader

We don't love qualities, we love a person; sometimes by reason of their defects as well as their qualities.

—*JACQUES MARITAIN (1882-1973)*
French philosopher

In love you find the oddest combinations: Materialistic people find themselves in love with idealists. Clingers fall in love with players; . . . homebodies capture and try to smother butterflies. If it weren't so serious we could laugh at it.

—GEORGE DAVIS, *b. 1939*
American writer & teacher

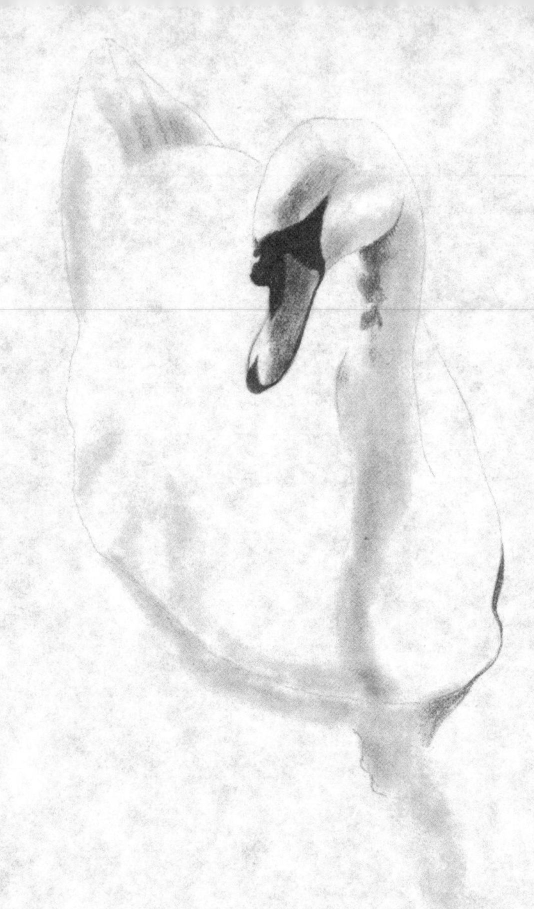

. . . I was at a party feeling very shy because there were a lot of celebrities around, and I was sitting in a corner alone and a very beautiful young man came up to me and offered me some salted peanuts and he said, "I wish they were emeralds" as he handed me the peanuts and that was the end of my heart. I never got it back.

—HELEN HAYES, *b. 1900*
American actress

. . . if we never met again in our lives I should feel that somehow the whole adventure of existence was justified by my having met you.

—*LEWIS MUMFORD, b. 1895*
American writer, & historian

Love is like a pair of socks—you have to have two, and they gotta match.

—ANONYMOUS

Love is an irresistible desire to be irresistibly desired.

—*ROBERT FROST (1874-1963)*
American poet

The great tragedy of life is not that men perish, but that they cease to love.

—*W. SOMERSET MAUGHAM (1874-1965)*
English writer

To fear love is to fear life . . .

—*BERTRAND RUSSELL (1872-1970)*
English mathematician & philosopher

The course of true love never did run smooth.

—*WILLIAM SHAKESPEARE (1564-1616)*
English dramatist & poet

Love comforteth like sunshine after rain.

—*WILLIAM SHAKESPEARE (1564-1616)*
English dramatist & poet

Oh, life is a glorious cycle of song,
A medley of extemporanea;
And love is a thing that can never go wrong;
And I am Marie of Roumania.

—*DOROTHY PARKER (1893-1967)*
American writer

All love is sweet,
Given or returned.

—*PERCY BYSSHE SHELLEY (1792-1822)*
English poet

Hearts are not had as a gift but hearts are earned . . .

—*WILLIAM BUTLER YEATS (1865-1939)*
Irish poet & dramatist

How bold one gets when one is sure of being loved!

—*SIGMUND FREUD (1856-1939)*
Austrian; founder of psychoanalysis

Love is the most subtle form of self-interest.

—*HOLBROOK JACKSON (1874-1948)*
English literary scholar & editor

Love is but the discovery of ourselves in others, and the delight in the recognition.

—*ALEXANDER SMITH (1830-1867)*
Scottish poet

Love looks not with the eyes, but with the mind . . .

—*WILLIAM SHAKESPEARE (1564-1616)*
English dramatist & poet

Wine comes in at the mouth; love comes in through the eye.

—*HENRI MATISSE (1869-1954)*
French artist

To love
is to receive a glimpse of heaven.

—*KAREN SUNDE, b. 1942*
American actor-playwright

How vast a memory has Love!

—*ALEXANDER POPE (1688-1744)*
English writer

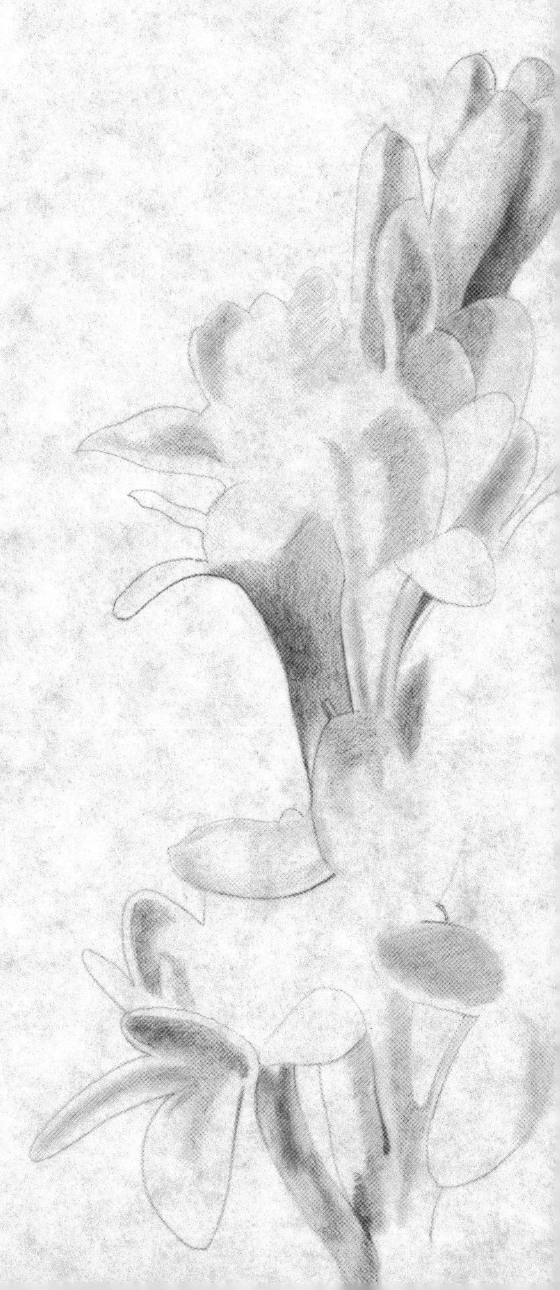

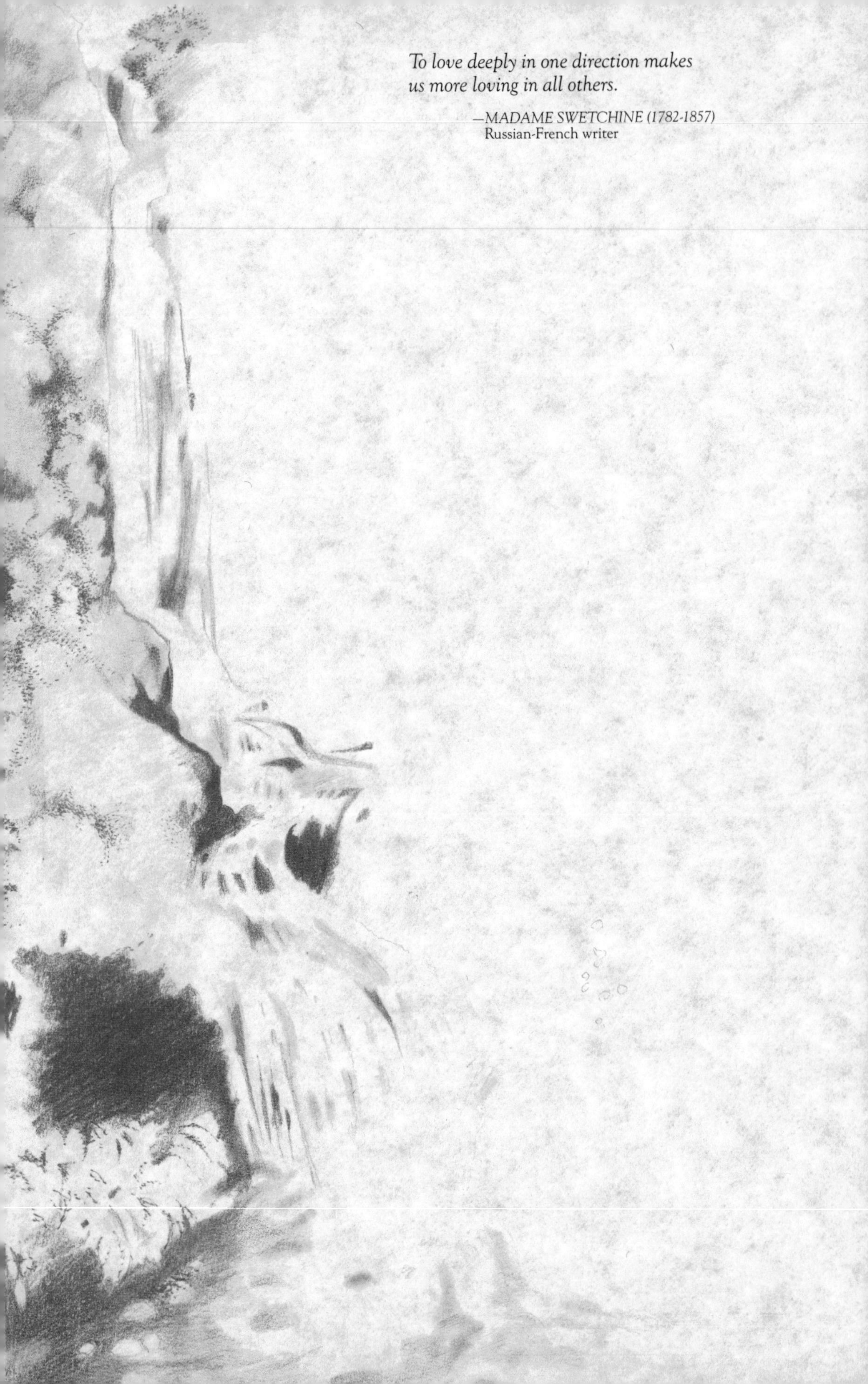

To love deeply in one direction makes us more loving in all others.

—*MADAME SWETCHINE (1782-1857)*
Russian-French writer

Life has taught us that love does not consist in gazing at each other but in looking outward together in the same direction.

—*ANTOINE DE SAINT EXUPÉRY (1900-1944)*
French writer

Between whom there is hearty truth there is love . . .

—*HENRY DAVID THOREAU (1817-1862)*
American writer

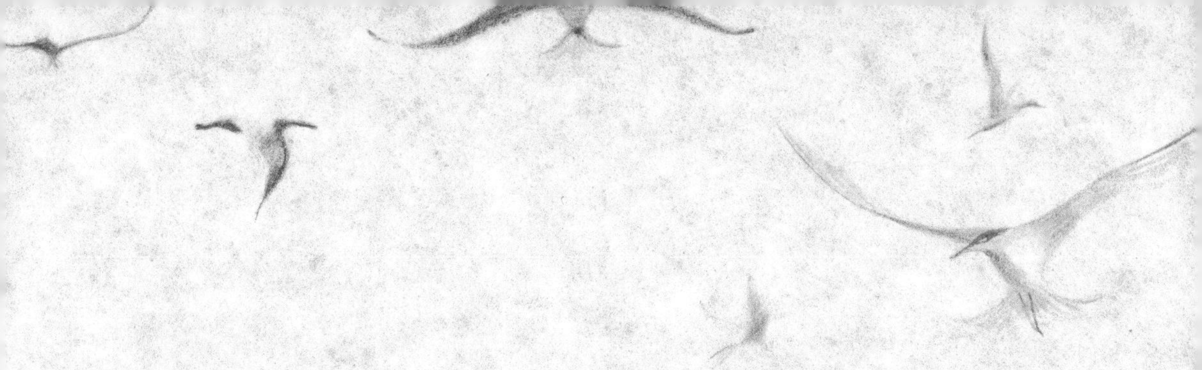

There is but one genuine love-potion—consideration.

—*MENANDER (342-292 B.C.)*
Greek playwright

Love is what you've been through with somebody.

—*JAMES THURBER (1894-1961)*
American writer & cartoonist

Love is not a matter of counting the years—it's making the years count.

—*WOLFMAN JACK SMITH*
American disc jockey

Where love reigns the impossible may be attained.

—INDIAN PROVERB

Love conquers all things . . .

—*VIRGIL (70-19 B.C.)*
Roman poet

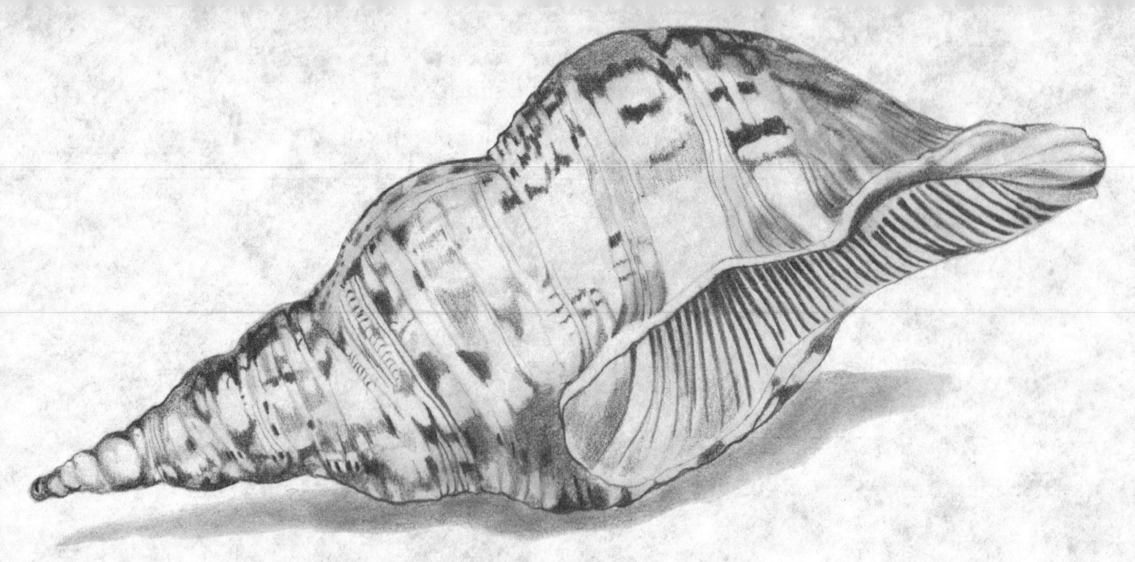

Without love intelligence is dangerous;
without intelligence love is not enough.

—*ASHLEY MONTAGU, b. 1905*
American anthropologist

Remember my unalterable maxim, "When we love, we always have something to say."

—*LADY MARY WORTLEY MONTAGU (1689-1762)*
English writer

My love for you is mixed throughout my body . . .

—*ANCIENT EGYPTIAN LOVE SONG*
(c. 1550-1080 B.C.)

I love thee with the breath,
Smiles, tears, of all my life!

—*ELIZABETH BARRETT BROWNING (1806-1861)*
English poet

The way to love anything is to realize that it might be lost.

—G.K. CHESTERTON *(1874-1936)*
English writer

He who is not impatient is not in love.

—ITALIAN PROVERB

Love is the triumph of imagination over intelligence.

—*H.L. MENCKEN (1880-1956)*
American writer

So, if I dream I have you, I have you,
For, all our joys are but fantastical.

—*JOHN DONNE (1572-1631)*
English poet

Love begets love. This torment is my joy.

—*THEODORE ROETHKE (1908-1963)*
American poet

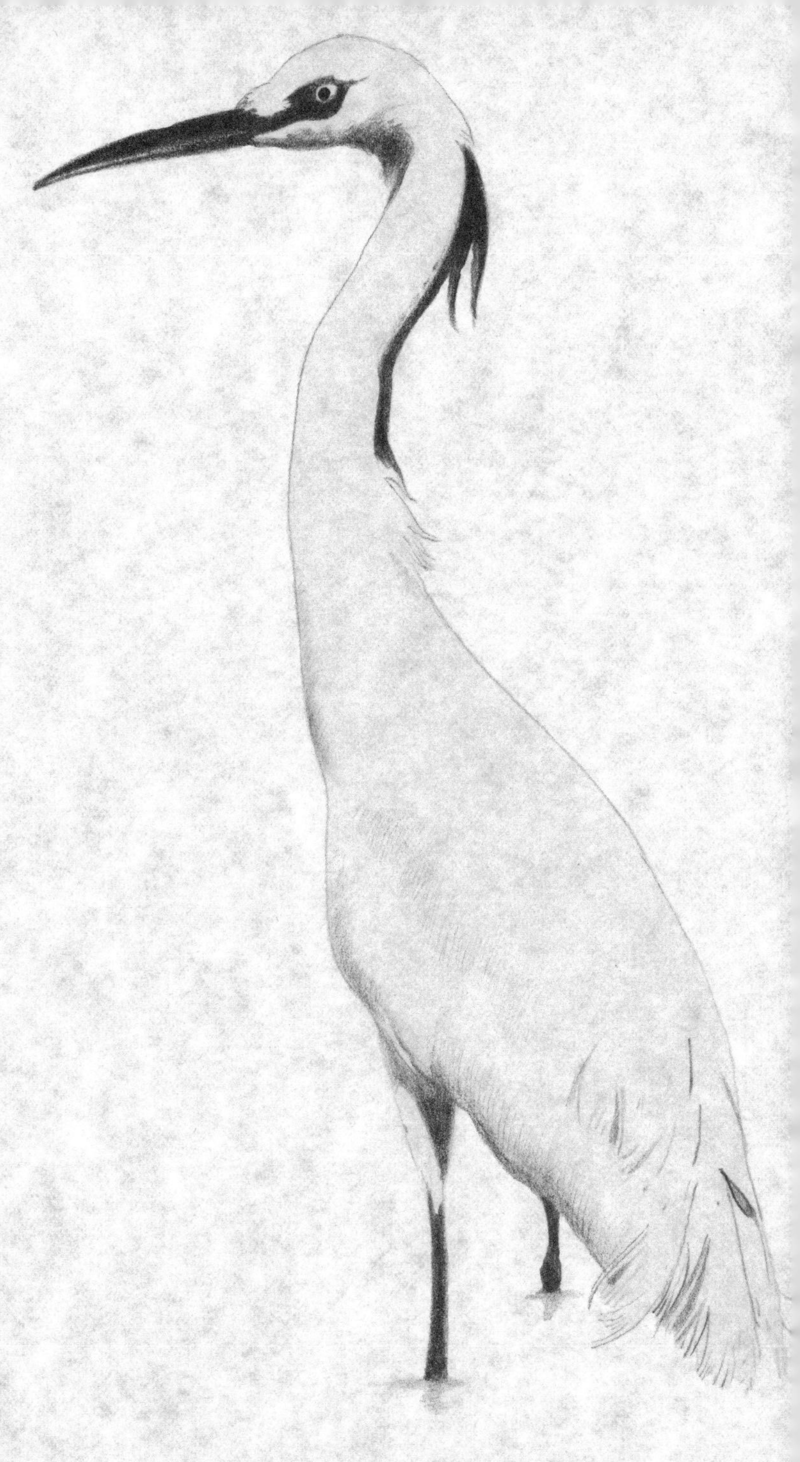

Love cures people—both the ones who give it and the ones who receive it.

—*DR. KARL MENNINGER, b. 1893*
American psychiatrist

Very fine is my valentine.
Very fine and very mine.

—*GERTRUDE STEIN (1874-1946)*
American poet

I would rather have a crust and a tent with you than be queen of all the world.

—*ISABEL BURTON (1831-1896)*
English writer

The loving are the daring.

—*BAYARD TAYLOR (1825-1878)*
American writer

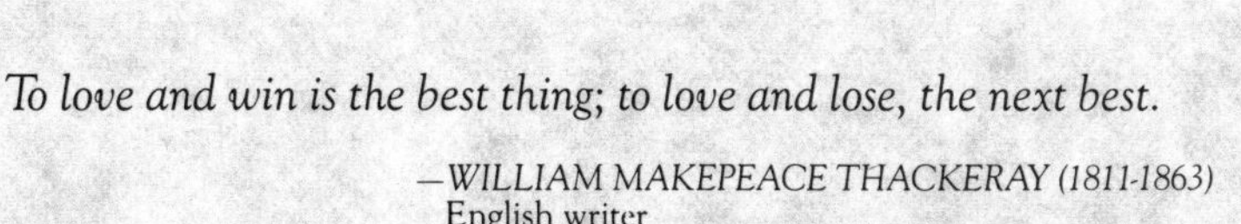

To love and win is the best thing; to love and lose, the next best.

—*WILLIAM MAKEPEACE THACKERAY (1811-1863)*
English writer

Love is an act of endless forgiveness, a tender look which becomes a habit.

—*PETER USTINOV, b. 1921*
English actor & writer

To get the full value of joy you must have someone to divide it with.

—*MARK TWAIN (1835-1910)*
American writer

Love is a hole in the heart.

—*BEN HECHT (1894-1964)*
American writer

Pains of love be sweeter far
Than all other pleasures are.

—*JOHN DRYDEN (1631-1700)*
English poet

Come live with me, and be my love,
And we will some new pleasures prove,
Of golden sands, and crystal brooks,
With silken lines, and silver hooks.

—*JOHN DONNE (1572-1631)*
English poet

Earth's the right place for love;
I don't know where it's likely to get better.

—*ROBERT FROST (1874-1963)*
American poet

There is only one happiness in life, to love and be loved.

—GEORGE SAND *(1804-1876)*
French writer

Love is . . . born with the pleasure of looking at each other, it is fed with the necessity of seeing each other, it is concluded with the impossibility of separation!

—*JOSÉ MARTÍ Y PERÉZ (1853-1895)*
Cuban writer

Love knoweth no laws.

—*SIR JOHN LYLY (1554?-1606)*
English writer